COOL COINS

Creating Fun *and* Fascinating Collections!

Pam Scheunemann

ABDO
Publishing Company

Visit us at
www.abdopublishing.com

Published by ABDO Publishing Company, 4940 Viking Drive, Edina, Minnesota 55435.
Copyright © 2007 by Abdo Consulting Group, Inc. International copyrights reserved in all countries.
No part of this book may be reproduced in any form without written permission from the publisher.
The Checkerboard Library™ is a trademark and logo of ABDO Publishing Company.

Printed in the United States.

Design and Production: Mighty Media, Inc.
Cover Photo: Anders Hanson
Interior Photos: Anders Hanson; Shutterstock; United States coin and production images courtesy
the United States Mint: United States Mint, United States Mint Proof Set, and United States Mint
Uncirculated Coin Set are registered trademarks of the United States Mint; quarter-dollar coin
images pp. 9, 18–19 from the United States Mint; images p. 23 courtesy Numismatic Guaranty
Corporation; lydian coins, p. 7, Reid Goldsborough.
Series Editor: Pam Price

Special thanks to Craig Johnson of Valley Coin (www.valleycoin.com) for his knowledge and
assistance.

Library of Congress Cataloging-in-Publication Data

Scheunemann, Pam, 1955-
  Cool coins / Pam Scheunemann.
     p. cm. -- (Cool collections)
  Includes index.
  ISBN-13: 978-1-59679-770-3
  ISBN-10: 1-59679-770-3
 1. Coins--Collectors and collecting--Juvenile literature. I. Title. II. Series: Cool collections
     (Edina, Minn.)

CJ89.S34 2006
332.63--dc22   2006011960

Contents

It's Time for Change 4

A Brief History of Coins 6

The Elements of a Coin 8

Making Money 10

How to Get Started 12

Collecting U.S. Coins 15

Do Your Homework 20

Adding to Your Collection 24

Caring for Your Collection 26

Conclusion 30

Glossary 31

Web Sites 31

Index 32

It's Time for Change

CHANGE. IT'S SOMETHING YOU PROBABLY HANDLE EVERY DAY. Do you ever take the time to stop and look at the pennies, nickels, dimes, and quarters you have? We see coins every day, so it's easy to overlook the history of the works of art we just call change.

The cool thing about collecting coins is that you can start with what's in your pocket. Look closely. How many of these coins have different dates? Which coins are in good condition? Do you wonder where they were made or what they are made of? If you find a really old coin, is it worth more than just the **face value**? Before you know it, you're hooked!

U.S. Quarter

Japanese Yen

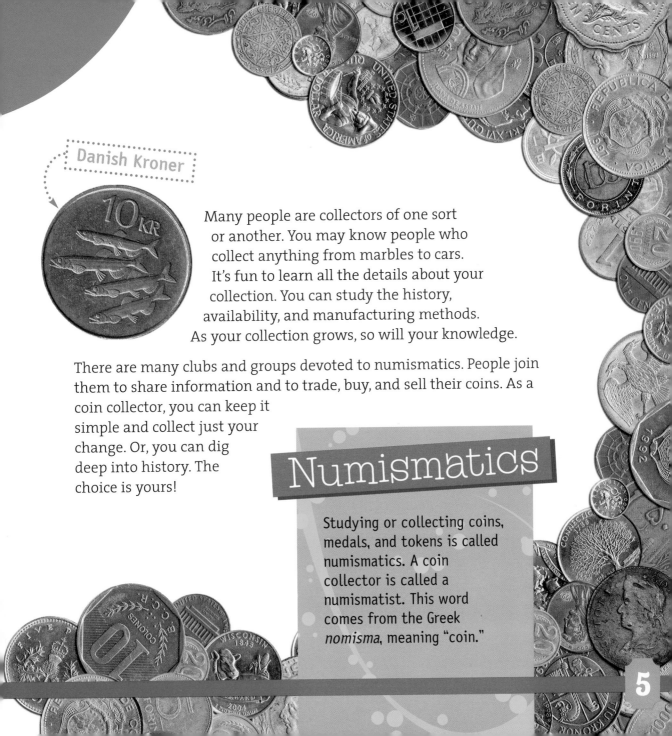

Danish Kroner

10 KR

Many people are collectors of one sort or another. You may know people who collect anything from marbles to cars. It's fun to learn all the details about your collection. You can study the history, availability, and manufacturing methods. As your collection grows, so will your knowledge.

There are many clubs and groups devoted to numismatics. People join them to share information and to trade, buy, and sell their coins. As a coin collector, you can keep it simple and collect just your change. Or, you can dig deep into history. The choice is yours!

Numismatics

Studying or collecting coins, medals, and tokens is called numismatics. A coin collector is called a numismatist. This word comes from the Greek *nomisma*, meaning "coin."

A Brief History of Coins

THROUGHOUT THE AGES, PEOPLE HAVE TRADED WHAT THEY HAD AVAILABLE FOR GOODS AND SERVICES. Some of the earliest forms of currency were beads, shells, tools, livestock, food, and cloth. These things were not always readily available. And, they were often difficult to carry around. Can you imagine bringing a sheep or a chicken every time you wanted to trade for something?

Eventually, people began using **precious metals** for currency. Yet this was difficult. For each transaction, the metals had to be weighed and tested for purity. Then, around 600 BC, the Lydians made the first coins containing gold. They used electrum, an **alloy** of gold and silver, to make small, bean-shaped lumps of equal weight. Then, these coins were stamped with an official symbol.

The use of coins spread quickly to other regions, which each made their own coins. Many ancient Greek and Roman cities issued their own coins. Early coins had designs hammered into them. Animals, insects, and vegetables were some of the earliest designs.

Over time, the lumpy bean shapes were transformed into the flat, circular shape we know today. This shape was better suited to display **intricate** designs. Images of important rulers, gods, goddesses, historical events, or other symbols appeared on the coins. People viewed the coins as things of beauty. And, people wanted their city's coins to be the most impressive. The work of **engravers** was elevated to an art form. Artists even began to sign their work.

U.S. coins are not too different from ancient coins. They also feature symbols and historical figures. Each coin has a history of its own. Coins are a link to the past, whether ancient or recent.

The Elements of a Coin

Legend

The lettering on the coin.

Field

The part of the coin that does not contain any pictures or words.

Edge

The outside rim around the coin. It is sometimes called the third side of the coin. The edge may be reeded, which means it has small lines on it.

Inscription

Any words, letters, phrases, or numbers on a coin.

Bust

A portrait on the coin that shows a person from the shoulders up.

Artist/Designer

The initials of the person who created the coin's design. On the one-cent coin, VDB stands for Victor D. Brenner.

Relief

The part of the design that is raised above the field.

Date

The year the coin was minted.

Mint Mark

A small letter on the coin that indicates which mint produced the coin.

Rim

The raised area around the inside edge of a coin on both sides. This rim protects the coin's design from wear.

Heads or Tails?

You've probably tossed a coin and called heads or tails. These terms refer to the obverse and reverse sides of a coin.

Obverse is the front side of a coin. Since the obverse side often displays a bust of a person, this side became known as heads. The obverse side of most coins also displays the date and main design. However, the new 50 State Quarters® are an exception.

Reverse is the back, or tails, side of the coin.

Mint Marks

A mint mark is a letter stamped onto a coin. It tells where the coin was minted. Current U.S. coins are minted in Philadelphia, Pennsylvania (P), and Denver, Colorado (D). Coins without a mint mark are also made in Philadelphia. San Francisco, California (S), and West Point, New York (W), mint only coins for collectors.

Inscriptions

Federal law currently requires that all U.S. coins bear the year of issue, the denomination of the coin, and a mint mark. They must also bear certain inscriptions. These are:

- In God We Trust

- Liberty

- United States of America

- *E Pluribus Unum*, which is Latin for "out of many, one"

Making Money

THE UNITED STATES MINT WAS ESTABLISHED IN 1792.
That is when Congress passed the Coinage Act. The first mint was located in Philadelphia. The first coins it produced were copper cents dated 1793. Before then, the colonists used many different types of coins.

1 The design is the first of several steps in making circulating coins. Circulating coins are the coins we use every day. Once Congress authorizes a new coin design, an artist creates the art for the coin. The artist makes the design very big so all the details can be seen.

2 Then, a clay model is made from the drawing. This model is much larger than the actual coin. It is the base for a series of casts.

3 The next step is pouring plaster over the clay model. At this point, all the details are refined and another plaster is made. It is sent to the lab of the United States Mint for final approval.

4 The final cast is made of a hard **epoxy**. A transfer-engraving machine traces the epoxy cast and reduces the design to the final size. Then, a special tool cuts the reduced design into a tool called the master **hub**.

5 The master hub is the first in a series of dies and hubs that create the final working **dies**. The dies come in pairs. There is one for the obverse and one for the reverse of each coin.

6 The coins start out as a long sheet of metal. This sheet is run through a circle-cutting machine. It works similar to a cookie cutter, punching out round blanks. The excess metal is melted down and reused.

7 The blanks are heated to soften them. Next, they are washed. Then, they are placed in a machine that raises a rim on both sides of the blanks. This machine is called the upsetting mill. After this process, the coin blanks are called planchets.

8 The coin press is the next step. It uses thousands of pounds of pressure to press the dies into both sides of the planchets. Finally, the coins are checked for quality and sent to a Federal Reserve bank for circulation.

How to Get Started

IT'S NOT HARD TO START A COIN COLLECTION. After all, coins are part of our everyday lives. However, a collection is more than just a jar of coins. Gathering, organizing, categorizing, preserving, and displaying a specific set of coins makes a collection.

Sometimes it seems difficult to know just how to start a collection. You can start with your own pocket change. Ask friends and relatives if they have old change you can go through. As you pick up each coin, look at its design. Check the date and the mint mark. Is the coin in good condition, or does it have a lot of scratches?

Soon, you will notice the minor differences in the coins. It is certain that some coins will catch your eye. Those are the coins that will start your collection!

A Series Collection

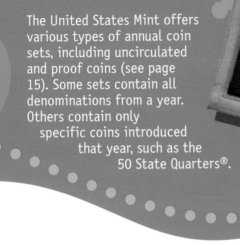

The United States Mint offers various types of annual coin sets, including uncirculated and proof coins (see page 15). Some sets contain all denominations from a year. Others contain only specific coins introduced that year, such as the 50 State Quarters®.

Types of Collections

There are many types of coin collections. There is no right or wrong way to collect coins.

SERIES COLLECTION

A series collection is based on one specific denomination. It contains a coin of that denomination from each mint and each year the coin was minted.

TYPE SET

A type set is a collection of all the major designs used for each denomination. This can be expanded upon by including variations of each design type.

DATE COLLECTION

A date collection includes all the coins minted in a specific year. For example, a penny, a nickel, a dime, a quarter, a half-dollar, and a dollar from the year you were born is a date collection.

Theme collection

There are coins and various medals that have a specific theme, such as presidents or birds. You can collect whatever interests you.

The U.S. presidents appear on many coins. This is an example of a theme collection.

Foreign coins

Foreign coins can be collected in a number of ways. You can collect one country's coins in various **denominations**. You can also collect foreign coins by theme or historical event.

Ancient coins

Ancient coins were made individually by hand. These coins are not uniform and round like modern coins.

Collecting U.S. Coins

YOUR COIN COLLECTION CAN BE STARTED FROM CIRCULATING COINS, BOTH OLD AND NEW. The United States Mint also makes several special coins for numismatists.

Uncirculated Coins

An uncirculated coin is in new condition and does not show any signs of wear. The United States Mint also produces uncirculated coins that are meant to be collected. They are similar to circulating coins. But, they have several quality improvements. Uncirculated coins receive special cleaning and packaging after they are stamped.

A first day cover contains a coin from each mint. It is postmarked with the date of release to the public.

Proof Coins

Proof coins are specially minted. They are made specifically for collectors. Proof coins are stamped at least twice to give the coin sharper detail. Some proof coins are highly processed so the field has a mirrorlike finish. The relief areas may be in either a satin or a glossy finish.

Some proof coins are made of silver. Others are made out of the same materials as circulating coins. Proof coins are placed in protective packaging.

Medals

Medals may resemble coins, but they have no value as money. They are created to honor a person or a historical event. The United States Mint produces commemorative, presidential, mint, and treasury medals. There are also private mints that produce medals and commemorative coins. However, only the United States Mint can produce coins that are legal tender in the United States.

Commemorative Coins

Commemorative coins are special coins minted to honor a person, an organization, or an event. They are not typically circulating coins. Commemorative coins are ordinarily minted in limited numbers. These coins are sold to raise money for monuments, expositions, Olympics, and the like. There are some commemorative coins made for circulation, such as the coins in the 50 State Quarters® program.

Legal Tender

Legal tender is official money that is valid as payment toward a debt and that a creditor must accept.

Bullion Coins

Precious metals in the form of bars, **ingots**, or coins are called bullion. Buying bullion coins is a way to invest. Many countries and private mints produce bullion coins. Each United States Mint bullion coin has a **denomination** on it. However, these coins are usually sold by their weight, such as one ounce (28 g), one-half ounce (14 g), one-quarter ounce (7 g), and one-tenth ounce (3 g).

As precious metals go up and down in price, the value of bullion coins changes. When buying a bullion coin, you may pay a small amount over its basic value. This covers the manufacturing and handling fees. The United States Mint makes American Eagle bullion coins. Each of these coins has a **face value** printed on it and can be used as legal tender. However, their face value is mostly symbolic. Typically, they are worth more.

The United States Mint also makes gold, silver, and platinum proof coins. These coins are produced with the high quality of other proof coins. They are created especially for numismatic purposes.

The silver American Eagle proof coin features *Walking Liberty*, the 1916–1947 half-dollar design. It is available only in one-ounce (28-g) coins. It has a face value of $1.

State Quarters

The 50 State Quarters® program started in 1999 and runs through 2008. Five quarters are issued each year for ten years. Each quarter has the same obverse design showing George Washington. The reverse designs may include **landmarks**, historical buildings, symbols of resources or industries, plants, or animals related to the state. It's a great way to start a collection and learn a bit about each state along the way!

50 State Quarters® Program Schedule

1999	Delaware, Pennsylvania, New Jersey, Georgia, Connecticut	2004	Michigan, Florida, Texas, Iowa, Wisconsin
2000	Massachusetts, Maryland, South Carolina, New Hampshire, Virginia	2005	California, Minnesota, Oregon, Kansas, West Virginia
2001	New York, North Carolina, Rhode Island, Vermont, Kentucky	2006	Nevada, Nebraska, Colorado, North Dakota, South Dakota
2002	Tennessee, Ohio, Louisiana, Indiana, Mississippi	2007	Montana, Washington, Idaho, Wyoming, Utah
2003	Illinois, Alabama, Maine, Missouri, Arkansas	2008	Oklahoma, New Mexico, Arizona, Alaska, Hawaii

Colorized Coins and Medals

There are several companies that colorize images on coins and medals. Some of the colorization is done on actual United States Mint coins. Others may be **replicas** and should be marked as such on the coin. The quarters in the 50 State Quarters® program are popular colorized coins to collect.

These are just a few of the reverse designs of the 50 State Quarters®.

Do Your Homework

READ, READ, READ! BEFORE
YOU RUN OUT AND SPEND ANY
MONEY, IT IS IMPORTANT TO DO SOME RESEARCH.
Sounds like work, doesn't it? Well surprisingly, the more you
learn, the more you'll want to learn! You will find a lot of
interesting answers when you research coins.

Each type of coin has a **unique** history. That's part of what makes
coins interesting and valuable to a collector. The Internet is a great
place to get information about a coin or about coin collecting in
general. As you dig around various numismatic Web sites, you'll
get a feel for what interests you.

Books are also a good source of information. There are many books
about collecting coins that can help you expand your knowledge.
It is also very important for a collector to have a pricing guide.
Pricing guides with up-to-date coin pricing are published
annually.

There are also numismatic clubs and associations that you can
join. You can gain a lot of knowledge from people who already
collect coins. Attend a local coin show. There will be many dealers
and collectors there who love to share their tales of numismatics.
There is nothing like hands-on learning.

Handling Coins

Because they are made of metal, you may think that coins are indestructible. That is not the case. To keep coins in perfect condition, you must treat them as if they were as delicate as glass. One tiny nick or scratch on a coin can seriously reduce its value. So, it is a good idea to handle your coins over a soft, padded surface, such as a folded piece of cloth.

First and foremost, always hold a coin by its edges. A tiny piece of dirt on a finger can cause a scratch. And, the oils in your skin can discolor the metal. The discoloration may not show up immediately, but it will over time. And, it will be permanent.

Coins should always be kept dry. Even the moisture in your breath can cause spotting on a coin.

Be respectful when handling coins, especially uncirculated and proof coins. Proof coins may come in plastic protective cases. It is best to leave them in their cases! Wear white cotton gloves when handling valuable coins.

Grading Coins

One aspect of collecting coins is knowing their values. Whether you are buying or selling, you need to know the value of the coin. Each person may look at a coin's condition differently, and therefore value it differently. Over the years, a grading scale has been developed to make the definitions of the grades as standard as possible.

Grade is determined by looking at the strike, wear, luster, and eye appeal of the coin. Strike is a measure of how well the planchet was struck with the **dies**. It is determined by the quality of the die and the pressure used to make the impressions on the coin.

The wear of a coin is just that. What condition is the coin in? Are the details crisp, or have they worn off? Are there any scratches or discolored areas?

Luster describes the way light reflects off the surface of the coin. It's sort of like being shiny instead of dull. However, even though some proof coins have a satin finish, they will still have a luster.

And, of course, there's eye appeal. Does the overall coin look good? Is the type still readable?

Grading Terms

Here are definitions of the major grades. Each grade can be further defined by subcategories using a numerical scale. It takes a lot of study and experience to precisely grade coins. Even with experience, different people may grade the same coin differently. But, it's good to be familiar with the terms.

Uncirculated (Unc or MS). MS stands for mint state, no trace of wear.

About Uncirculated (AU-50). Original luster, only very slight traces of wear.

Extremely Fine (EF-40). Detail is complete, a bit of luster showing.

Very Fine (VF-20). Some wear on high points of the design, all lettering is sharp.

Fine (F-12). Moderate wear, all type readable, design is bold and showing some detail.

Very Good (VG-8). Well worn, the features are clear but without a lot of detail.

Good (G-4). Worn, but the design elements are still faintly visible.

About Good (AG-3). Heavily worn, type and date are somewhat readable.

Fair (FR-2). Very heavily worn, some details and date visible.

Poor (PO-1). Mostly worn down so that you can't read the date and other type, surface is smooth.

Fine   Very Fine   Extremely Fine   About Uncirculated   Mint State

Adding to Your Collection

NOW THAT YOU'RE ARMED WITH SOME KNOWLEDGE ABOUT COINS, YOU'RE READY TO BEGIN YOUR COLLECTION OR ADD TO THE COINS YOU ALREADY HAVE. There are many ways you can do this.

1. Check change jars around your house.

2. Ask relatives or friends, especially older ones, if you can look through their change jars.

3. Go to your local bank and purchase rolls of coins to sort through.

4. Visit coin dealers in your area.

5. Attend coin shows where you can shop from several dealers at one time.

6. Buy coin-related publications. Many of these have advertisements for coins available by mail order.

7. Purchase coins from the United States Mint. It offers proof and uncirculated coins for sale.

8. Search the Internet. You can find all types of coins available online.

9. Visit flea markets and antique shows. These events sometimes have coins for sale.

What You See Is What You Get

It is important to thoroughly examine coins before you buy them. You can often see the date and type on a coin with your eyes. But to get a really good look at the condition of a coin, you'll need a magnifier. This tool will help you see scratches or small dents that may be in the coin's surface.

Safe Buying Tips

- Know as much as you can about a coin before you buy it. Read about the history of the coin. Is it rare, or is it readily available?

- Determine how much you will spend before you purchase a coin. Check out the current price for the coin you want to buy.

- Become familiar with the dealers in your area. Once you get to know the dealers, select one you trust.

- It is a good idea to purchase from a dealer who has a return policy. Be sure to ask about the return policy before you buy.

- If the deal seems too good to be true, it probably is. Do your research. If the seller is asking too little, the coin may not actually be what it seems to be.

Storage

Proper storage is necessary to protect your coins. It is important to keep your coins dry. Moisture can damage coins. To avoid scratches and dents, you also must prevent coins from rubbing against each other. There are many different types of storage devices available for coins. When you visit your local coin dealer, be sure to look at various storage options.

2 X 2 CARDBOARD HOLDERS are a popular and inexpensive choice for storage. These holders are made of cardboard lined with a thin, plastic film called Mylar®. There are different-sized holes to fit a variety of coins. Place the coin inside, and then fold over and staple the cardboard. Be sure to turn down the edges of the staples so they don't scratch other coins when the holders are stacked.

There are several advantages to cardboard holders. You can easily write information about the coin on the holder. And no matter the size of the coin, each holder is the same size. This means the holders can be stored in a row, and it will be easy to flip through them.

2 x 2 VINYL HOLDERS are called flips. Their advantages are similar to those of cardboard holders. They have two pockets. One is for the coin and one is for the coin's description. It is important that the vinyl used to make the holder does not contain polyvinyl chloride, or PVC. This chemical can damage coins.

HARD-PLASTIC HOLDERS come in different styles. Clear cases are relatively inexpensive and will hold a single coin. This type of case can be bulky and will not stand up in a box. Other plastic holders are shaped like the 2 x 2 cardboard holders and consist of three layers of hard plastic. Hard-plastic holders are mostly used for more valuable coins.

PAPER ENVELOPES can be used for circulating coins. Be sure to get those made especially for coins. Regular envelopes contain chemicals that can harm coins over time.

PAPER ROLLS can be used for storing circulating coins. However, they may discolor the coins over time.

SLABS are hard-plastic containers that coins are sealed in by a professional grading service. A piece of paper that identifies the coin and its grade certification is also sealed inside it. Having a coin slabbed is expensive. This method of storage is typically used only for rare and valuable coins.

COIN ALBUMS come in a variety of shapes, sizes, and materials. Paper folders designed to hold one type of coin set, such as the 50 State Quarters®, are especially popular. These should be used for circulation-quality coins. They are a simple way to store and display your coins. You can easily see which coins you need to complete your collection.

There are also plastic pages that fit into a three-ring binder. The slots in the pages are the size of a 2 x 2 holder. You can put a coin in a holder and slide it into the plastic sleeve without stapling it.

PLASTIC TUBES are a quick and easy way to store a single **denomination** of coins. Tubes are used for circulating coins. They do not offer the protection of a single coin holder.

BOXES can be used to store individual holders. There are boxes specially made to hold 2 x 2 holders. Cardboard boxes, such as shoe boxes, have chemicals in them that can damage coins. A better solution is a plastic box with a tight-fitting lid. This will also keep out moisture.

Record Keeping

You may want to keep records of where and when you bought a coin and how much you paid for it. There are various coin-collecting computer programs available. You can also keep track of your collection in a word processing or spreadsheet program. Or, just use a journal. There are certain facts to record about each coin.

- Denomination
- Year
- Mint
- Grade
- Value

- Purchase date
- Type
- Quantity
- Cost
- Vendor

Cleaning Coins: Just Don't

You may find an old coin and think it would look good if it were cleaned. Well, experts say not to clean your coins. Cleaning coins can actually damage the surface of the coins. Coins with altered surfaces are worth less to collectors.

Toning refers to the shading of color on coins. What is called tarnish on silver is called toning on coins. The metals in coins react to different things in the atmosphere. Chemical reactions cause the coins to take on a different shading. Sometimes this shading is considered desirable by a collector. It can actually add value to some coins. Other coins will have an undesirable toning.

If you feel the need to clean a coin, be very careful. Do not use anything abrasive, such as silver polish, toothpaste, or an eraser. Use a mild soap and gently clean the coin. Strong soaps can give coins an unnatural, washed-out look. This can reduce the coin's value. Coins are works of art, and the cleaning should be left to a professional.

Conclusion

This book has only touched on the major points of numismatics. There is an endless wealth of information and history that surrounds coin collecting. Just start simply, and let your interests lead you from there. Read, ask questions, collect, and enjoy!

Glossary

alloy – a mixture of metals.

denomination – one of a series of kinds, sizes, or values of currency or weights.

die – an engraved metal piece used for stamping a pattern into a surface.

engraver – a person who carves or etches a design into clay, metal, or other material.

epoxy – a strong resin that hardens when exposed to heat and does not shrink much as it cures.

face value – the value indicated on the face of something, such as a coin or a stamp.

hub – a steel device from which a die is produced.

ingot – metal formed into a shape that is easy to handle or store.

intricate – having parts that are arranged in a complex or elaborate manner.

landmark – a building or place that is chosen and pointed out as important.

precious metal – a metal that is high in value, such as silver, gold, or platinum.

replica – a copy of something.

unique – unlike anything else.

Web Sites

To learn more about cool coins, visit ABDO Publishing Company on the World Wide Web at **www.abdopublishing.com.** Web sites about cool coins are featured on our Book Links page. These links are routinely monitored and updated to provide the most current information available.

Index

A

alloy 6, 31

ancient coins 7, 14

B

bullion coins 17

C

cardboard holders 26, 27

commemorative coins 16

currency 6

D

date collection 13

denomination 9, 13, 17, 28, 29, 31

dies 11, 22

F

face value 4, 17, 31

50 State Quarters® 9, 13, 16, 18, 19, 28

foreign coins 14

G

grading coins 22

H

handling coins 21

hard-plastic holders 27

I

ingots 17, 31

M

making money 10, 11

medals 5, 14, 16, 19

N

numismatics 5, 17, 20

P

paper envelopes 27

paper rolls 27

planchets 11

precious metals 6, 17, 31

proof coins 13, 15, 17, 21, 22

S

satin finish 15, 22

series collection 12, 13

slabs 27

T

theme collection 14

type set 13

U

uncirculated coins 15, 24

United States Mint 10, 13, 15, 16, 17, 19, 24

V

vinyl holders 27